REAL LIFE HEROES

SURVIVING
NATURAL DISASTERS

REAL LIFE HEROES

SURVIVING NATURAL DISASTERS

Jen Green

ARCTURUS

This edition first published in 2010 by Arcturus Publishing
Distributed by Black Rabbit Books
P.O. Box 3263
Mankato
Minnesota MN 56002

Printed in China

Series concept: Alex Woolf
Editors: Alex Woolf and Sean Connolly
Picture research: Alex Woolf
Designer: Ian Winton

Library of Congress Cataloging-in-Publication Data

Green, Jen.
  Surviving natural disasters / Jen Green.
     p. cm. -- (Real life heroes)
  Includes bibliographical references and index.
  ISBN 978-1-84837-693-9 (library binding) 4361 1002 11/10
  1. Natural disasters--Juvenile literature. 2. Natural disasters--Anecdotes. 3. Survival skills--Juvnile
literature. 4. Survival skills--Anecdotes. I. Title.
  GB5019.G733 2011
  363.34'9--dc22
                            2010014191

Picture Credits
Corbis: cover (Peter Turnley), 8 (Chen Xie/Xinhua Press), 9 (Altaf Hussain/Reuters), 10 (Jacques
Langevin/Sygma), 11 (Jacques Langevin/Sygma), 12 (Thierry Orban/Corbis Sygma), 13 (Peter Turnley),
14–15 (Yann Arthus-Bertrand), 16 (Michael S Yamashita), 17 (Hashimoto Noboru/Corbis Sygma), 19 (Yuriko
Nakao/Reuters), 20 (Beawiharta/Reuters), 21 (Nayan Sthankiya), 24 (Ryan Pyle), 25 (Michael
Reynolds/epa), 30 (St Louis Post/Corbis Sygma), 31 (Eric Nguyen), 32 (Jeff Mitchell/Reuters), 33 (Menno
Boermans/Aurora Photos), 35 (US Air Force/Science Faction), 36 (David Howells), 37 (Carlos
Barria/Reuters), 38 (Abir Abdullah/epa).
Getty Images: 22 (Jimin Lai/AFP), 27 (Topical Press Agency), 28 (Thomas D McAvoy/Time & Life Pictures),
40 (Roberto Schmidt/AFP), 41 (Roberto Schmidt/AFP), 42 (Paul Crock/AFP), 43 (Luis Ascui).
Science Photo Library: 7 (Gary Hincks).
Shutterstock: 6 (juliengrondin).

Cover picture: An Armenian girl recovers in hospital after being injured by a severe earthquake.

SL001051US   Supplier 03 Date 0510

Contents

Introduction

Planet Earth provides for all our needs. It gives us air to breathe, fresh water, and food. But the natural world can also be dangerous. Throughout Earth's history there have been natural disasters, such as earthquakes, volcanic eruptions, hurricanes, floods, and drought. Every year, natural disasters cause massive damage and kill many thousands of people. However, there are always survivors. These people have dramatic stories to tell of hardship, courage, and endurance.

Earthquakes and volcanoes

Earthquakes and volcanic eruptions are caused by immensely powerful forces within Earth. They are triggered by the movement of the huge rigid sections, called tectonic plates, that make up the planet's outer crust (see panel). As these plates shift, the ground heaves in an earthquake. Or molten rock from deep underground may burst onto the surface in a volcanic eruption. These natural hazards cause widespread destruction and may produce further dangers, such as landslides, avalanches, mudflows, fire, and floods. They can also send giant waves called tsunamis racing across the oceans.

▶ Lava spills from the crater of a volcano during an eruption. Most eruptions occur along the boundaries between tectonic plates, but red-hot rock may also erupt onto the surface through weak points called hot spots near the center of plates.

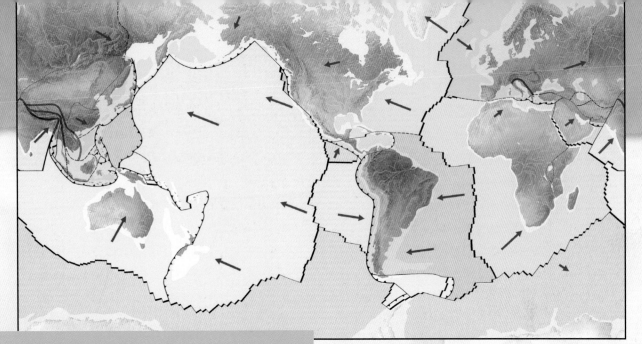

Tectonic jigsaw

Earth's outer crust is not one continuous layer, but is made up of around 30 sections called tectonic plates, which interlock like a planet-sized jigsaw. These sections ride on the red-hot layer below, called the mantle, like hunks of bread on a simmering soup. Slow-churning currents in the mantle set the plates drifting slowly across the globe, where they may clash together, scrape one another, or pull apart. Earthquakes are common along plate boundaries where plates grind past one another, putting rocks under tremendous strain. Where plates drift apart, either on land or on the seabed, molten rock surges upwards to form a volcano.

▲ This world map shows the Earth's tectonic plates. These plates may carry land, ocean, or both. The arrows show the direction of the plates' movement.

Extreme weather

Hurricanes, tornadoes, thunderstorms, and blizzards are types of extreme weather. Like all weather patterns, they are caused by the effects of the Sun's heat on the atmosphere and the oceans. Hurricanes are enormous whirling storms that form over warm oceans and can cause coastal flooding. Thunderstorms, tornadoes, and torrential rain can cause rivers to flood, while blizzards and heavy snow can produce avalanches. A drought is a long spell of dry weather, which can spark forest fires. Drought and other extreme weather can ruin crops and so produce famine—widespread hunger. Of all natural disasters, drought is one of the biggest killers, along with floods and earthquakes.

Survivors

Severe natural disasters can kill thousands of people. However, there are almost always survivors. These people are often called "lucky," yet most will suffer great hardship for months or even years to come. In the aftermath of a disaster, most survivors are shocked and bewildered by the scale of the destruction. They may be devastated by the loss of family and friends, or desperate to locate missing loved ones. Many will be injured. Most will have lost their homes and been forced to flee the disaster area with no time to gather possessions.

To the rescue

After a natural disaster strikes, the emergency services rush to the scene as quickly as possible. Help often arrives by air because transport links such as roads and railways are frequently damaged. Once on the scene, rescue workers comb the area for survivors. Medical staff treats the injured, and survivors are helped to safety. Nowadays rescue operations are often international efforts, with many countries sending experts and equipment such as bulldozers. As news of the disaster spreads, people all over the world help by giving money for food, clothing, shelter, and medicine. Gradually the stricken area is made safe, and services such as water and power are restored. Homes, factories, and offices are rebuilt.

In time survivors reach a place of safety, often sheltering in emergency camps. However, even here there may be little protection from severe weather, and food and clean water are often scarce. In these conditions disease can spread quickly. Survivors will usually have no means of earning a living to support their families and, at first, little or no access to services such as schools.

However upset by their ordeal, survivors are grateful for all the help they are given in the days, weeks, and months that follow. Aid organizations and charities provide food, medicine, and shelter. The government and armed forces help to restore essentials such as water and transport, and also law and order. Once the damage has been cleared, the work of rebuilding can begin. Eventually shops, offices, schools, and hospitals reopen, and people can often return to their home region if they wish. Normal life resumes, but the disaster will never be forgotten. However, with

◀ In 2008 a severe earthquake struck Sichuan province in central China. Many schools collapsed, trapping or killing students. Here a student helps a classmate trapped in the ruins of a high school.

▲ Victims of the Indian Ocean tsunami of December 26, 2004, wait in a refugee camp on India's remote Andaman and Nicobar Islands. Tsunamis raised by the earthquake off the coast of Indonesia swept over many of these low-lying islands and caused great destruction.

improvements to natural defences and early warning systems, survivors almost always hope that if a similar disaster strikes in future, the effects will be less severe.

Scientific study

People once believed that natural disasters were caused by bad luck or the anger of the gods. In the 20th century scientists made great progress in understanding the causes of earthquakes, eruptions, and other hazards. Sophisticated instruments were invented to monitor weather systems and sense earth movements in areas at risk of earthquakes. Powerful computers produce accurate forecasts of floods, droughts, and the effects of plate movement. If scientists believe that disaster is likely to strike immediately, the authorities issue a warning so the area can be evacuated (cleared of people). This saves many lives.

Nature is still more powerful than science. Scientists cannot control earthquakes, floods, hurricanes, and other natural hazards. However, careful planning can reduce the number of deaths. Aid donations can lessen the suffering of survivors and ease the long-term effects of disasters.

This book tells the stories of some young victims of natural disasters, the difficulties they encountered, and how they survived. The stories are all true, but people's names and some aspects of their identities have been changed.

Maia's Story

Armero, 1985

On November 13, 1985, the eruption of a snow-capped volcano in the Andes Mountains in South America caused a terrible disaster. Burning ash mixed with snow to produce a tide of mud that engulfed the town of Armero. Maia was one of only about 1,500 survivors from Armero, which had been home to 23,000 people.

In 1985 Armero was a prosperous town in a farming region. It lay on a fertile plain near the end of a narrow river canyon. The canyon led up to a high volcanic peak called Nevado del Ruiz. Twelve-year-old Maia lived in Armero with her parents and younger sister Dolores.

On the night of November 13 Maia had gone to bed as usual. Around midnight she was woken by a deep rumbling. She woke Dolores and rushed outside. The streetlights were out, but in the darkness Maia spotted what looked like a towering wall of mud surging down the street towards them.

Grabbing her sister's hand, Maia turned and fled. As they sprinted away they saw a tide of mud surging through the streets on either side, cutting off their escape. Maia made for a low hill not far away. Reaching the hill, they watched in horror as the swirling mud surrounded them on all sides. It rose to the roofs of houses below and then covered them. Shivering in their nightclothes, the sisters spent the night on the hill.

▶ An aerial view of the Andean town of Armero, which was obliterated by volcanic mudflows following the eruption of Nevado del Ruiz. After the disaster, Armero was abandoned and officially declared a cemetery. The town had been built on the site of a previous volcanic mudflow in 1845, which killed a thousand people, but this disaster had been forgotten.

Effects of volcanic eruptions

A volcano is a weak point in Earth's crust through which molten rock, ash, gas, and steam escape from deep underground. When Nevado del Ruiz erupted, burning ash and lava melted the mountain's snowy cap. Waves of mud surged down the narrow canyon to engulf Armero. Scientists had warned of the danger of mudflows when the volcano became active some weeks earlier, but the authorities failed to order evacuation.

As dawn broke Maia saw that the mud had set hard, trapping vehicles, fallen trees, and houses. Unknown to the sisters, the army and Red Cross had arrived in the night, but had to wait until dawn to search for survivors. It was afternoon before rescuers built a makeshift bridge to reach Maia and Dolores. They were taken by helicopter to the town of Guayabal, where a doctor dressed a cut on Maia's arm.

In the days that followed the sisters waited anxiously for news of their parents, but no news ever came. Their parents were among 21,500 people who died in Armero that night. The town was abandoned to the mud. Maia and Dolores spent months in a refugee camp and then moved in with a foster family. Maia later married and had two children of her own, but she has never forgotten the horror of that night.

▶ **A rescuer tries to free a child trapped in wreckage caused by the mudflows from Nevado del Ruiz. The death toll was among the highest ever caused by an eruption. All but 1,500 of the town's inhabitants were killed by the mudflows.**

Luke's Story
Lake Nyos, 1986

On August 21, 1986, a surge of poisonous gas from a volcanic lake in a remote part of Cameroon, West Africa, killed 1,700 people. The cloud of deadly gas from Lake Nyos engulfed three villages in a narrow valley leading down from the high lake. Luke, 14, was one of the first on the scene.

Lake Nyos is a deep crater lake located high on the slopes of an inactive volcano. Luke lived in a hilltop village nearby. Across the lake, a narrow wooded valley led to Nyos village, which was always busy on market day. On August 21 Luke's older brother, Nazarius, had gone to the market. He said he would stay with a friend overnight and return the next morning. But when he had not appeared by midday, Luke's mother sent him to fetch his brother.

◀ On August 21, 1986, the usually clear blue waters of Lake Nyos turned reddish-brown following the sudden release of poisonous gas that had built up at the bottom of the lake. Scientists found signs that a fountain of water and gas had washed over headlands edging the lake. The cloud of gas descended from the high lake, overwhelming people in nearby villages.

As Luke approached Nyos village, he realized something was wrong. The fields were deserted and no birds were singing. He met a herdsman and they entered the village together. There they witnessed a terrible sight. The narrow streets were strewn with the bodies of dogs, goats, and chickens. Luke spotted a man lying still in a doorway. Feeling scared he hurried to the friend's house. There he found the bodies of Nazarius and the friend's family. Luke desperately tried to revive his brother but failed.

▲ The cloud of poisonous carbon dioxide gas from Lake Nyos killed 1,700 villagers and thousands of livestock. The few survivors were resettled in villages a safe distance from the lake.

Luke stumbled out of the house and on through the streets. The scene everywhere was the same. Many people were lying dead in their beds. A stench like rotten eggs filled the air. At the far end of the village they at last found a survivor. The man told how, the previous evening, a strange cloud had appeared above the lake and flowed downhill to engulf the village. Finding it hard to breathe, the man had gone to bed and fallen unconscious.

Luke gave the survivor water and talked to him to keep him awake. Eventually rescuers arrived with oxygen. The few survivors were taken to the nearest hospital where they were treated for gas poisoning. Luke later learned that a cloud of poisonous gas from the lake had killed all but six of Nyos's inhabitants, and many people in nearby villages. Nyos village was abandoned, but Luke still lives quite near. He remains haunted by memories of that day.

What caused the Nyos disaster?

Soon after the disaster a team of American scientists visited Lake Nyos. They took samples from the lake and interviewed survivors. They decided that carbon dioxide gas seeping from underground had built up in the lake. When heavy rain or a small landslide disturbed the water, a huge bubble of gas had burst out of the lake and flowed downhill to Nyos. The village was sealed off, but in 2001 pipes were placed in the lake to release gas before it built up to dangerous levels.

Antonio's Story
Pinatubo, 1991

On June 15, 1991, a volcano called Pinatubo on an island in the Philippines began erupting violently. Ash shot high in the air, then settled in a thick layer over the countryside. After a severe storm, rainwater sent mud cascading down the mountain. The town of Bacolor, where 12-year-old Antonio lived with his family, lay directly in its path.

In 1991 Bacolor was a thriving town with 80,000 people. Antonio lived with his parents and two younger sisters next door to his grandparents. Just before the eruption began in June, the authorities ordered everyone to evacuate towns and villages within 18.5 miles of the mountain. But Bacolor lay outside the danger zone. Scientists warned of the risk of volcanic flows called lahars if heavy rain fell. However, the people of Bacolor felt safe because a high wall built to divert floodwater stood between them and the mountain.

On June 15 a violent eruption buried mountain slopes under thick ash. By September the eruption was dying down. But then a cyclone (tropical storm) struck the island at night. Torrential rain sent a tide of ash surging down a river bed towards Bacolor. The tide of slurry swept away the flood wall and roared on into town. Antonio's father, José, woke the family, who found themselves surrounded by thick, sticky mud.

Antonio and José helped the family onto the roof of their single-story home. From there they scrambled across a garage to the grandparents' house, which had two stories. They waited upstairs, but as the tide of mud rose higher, they used a drainpipe to climb onto the roof. Antonio helped his grandmother to safety. Torrential rain was still falling.

José now remembered his own uncle, who lived across the street. He cautiously lowered himself into the mud and found

▶ This aerial view shows the town of Bacolor, which was buried by a sea of mud and debris following the eruption of Pinatubo in June 1991. During a tropical storm torrential rain loosened a tide of ash and mud that swept down the mountain and into the town.

Types of eruption

There are several different types of eruption. The most dangerous is when a volcano explodes violently, as Pinatubo did in June 1991. The volcano shot a huge ash cloud high into the atmosphere, where it spread right around the world. However, thanks to prompt evacuation, only about 1,000 people died. Most of the victims were killed by lahars like the one that wiped out Bacolor.

he could keep afloat. José partly swam and partly slid across the lahar to his uncle's house and brought the old man back to the roof. Now several neighbors shouted for help. José made three more journeys to bring others to safety during that long, dark night.

By morning the rain had stopped and the mud stopped flowing. But the once-bustling town was buried beneath 20 feet of grey mud. Antonio and his family spent months in a refugee camp, before moving to a new house in the outskirts of the capital, Manila. Bacolor was mostly abandoned to the mud, though a few farming families still live there.

Tomi and Yoko's Story
Kobe, 1995

In January 1995 a powerful earthquake struck the Japanese port of Kobe, killing 6,300 people and making 30,000 people homeless. The city was badly damaged, not only by the quake but by the fires that followed. Tomi, a university student, witnessed the disaster. Her friend Yoko helped at a refugee center.

Kobe is a major port on the south coast of the Japanese mainland. In 1995 Tomi and Yoko were in their third year at Kobe University. Tomi lived with her parents in an apartment overlooking the bay. On January 17 an earthquake struck just offshore. Coastal parts of the city were the worst affected, but luckily the quake happened at 5.46 a.m., when most people were asleep.

▲ On January 17, 1995, the city of Kobe on the main Japanese island, Honshu, was struck by a severe earthquake. The damage was greatest in the parts of the city that bordered the ocean since the quake had struck offshore. These survivors are walking down a street littered with fallen debris and devastated by fire.

What happens in an earthquake?

The violent jolt of an earthquake releases pressure that has built up below ground as a result of tectonic plate movement. As plates slowly shift, rocks come under strain. When the pressure gets too great, rocks shatter and shock waves radiate through the ground. Most earthquakes strike deep below ground at a point called the focus. The damage is often worst on the surface directly above.

▲ When an earthquake strikes, people have no time to collect their possessions. They often escape with just the clothes they are wearing. These refugees from the Kobe earthquake of January 1995 are heating water over a brazier for a hot drink.

Tomi was woken by the shaking, which shattered glass and crockery. It also caused a power cut. In the darkness the family made their way downstairs. No one was injured and the damage was not too serious. Later Tomi left the house to walk to the shop where she worked part-time. Once outside she realized the scale of the disaster. Fires were burning fiercely across the city, and several buildings tilted at crazy angles. Cracks had appeared in roads and there was glass everywhere. The shop was also in chaos, with shelves tipped over. Tomi helped clear up the mess.

When she returned home, the power was back on. The family watched a news report on television. The quake had toppled the Hanshin Expressway, which had been built on tall pillars. Fires had been sparked by broken gas and electricity lines. Firefighters were struggling to put out the flames because water pipes were also broken.

Tomi's family had no water or gas for months. They had to fetch water in buckets for washing. They went to a neighbor's house to take a bath. The university was closed. After two days Tomi was able to telephone her friend Yoko, who lived in another part of the city. Yoko was also unhurt. Each expressed her joy that the other was unharmed. Two weeks later they were able to meet and hug one another.

Yoko lived with her family in northern Kobe, in the hills that edge the city. This district suffered less damage than the coast. Yoko decided to help those who had been less fortunate. She volunteered to help at a refugee center, which had been set up at a local school.

Yoko's first job was to take the names of the 600 refugees. She listened to stories of how people had survived the disaster. Some had been pulled from the ruins by soldiers sent in by the government to rescue survivors. Yoko also played with young children in the center. Many were still scared and in need of comfort.

Yoko's district still had water and gas. Her mother volunteered to wash the refugees' laundry. Yoko helped collect, sort, wash, and deliver the laundry. She continued to help at the center for three months until the university reopened. By that time gas and water supplies had been restored to much of the city. Rebuilding had begun. Both friends returned to university feeling that they had learned a lot about the importance of helping others.

Ring of Fire

Earthquakes mostly strike along deep cracks in Earth's crust called faults. These are mainly found along the edges of tectonic plates. Japan is located on the rim of the vast Pacific plate that lies below the Pacific Ocean. The rim of the Pacific plate runs right around the ocean. This vast, roughly circular plate border is called the Ring of Fire because earthquakes and volcanoes are common here.

George's Story
Indian Ocean Tsunami, 2004

On December 26, 2004, a violent earthquake rocked the seabed 149 miles west of Aceh province on the Indonesian island of Sumatra. The earthquake wrecked buildings in coastal towns and sent tsunamis racing across the ocean. George, a newly qualified nurse, witnessed what followed.

George lived in a coastal town in northern Aceh where he worked at a medical center. On December 26 a friend on a motorbike had picked him up early to go surfing. As they parked the bike at the beach, the ground began to shake violently. George and his friend lay flat as glass shattered, signs crashed down, and the bike fell over. The shaking continued for about 20 minutes. Some seafront buildings collapsed, but most remained standing.

When the shaking stopped, the pair got to their feet. People were screaming and sobbing. But George knew that worse might follow. From a magazine article he knew that undersea earthquakes could trigger giant waves called tsunamis. As they righted the motorbike, George urged his friend to carry them to the safety of the hills behind the town. He shouted for everyone to leave the coast.

▼ This photograph shows the devastation caused by the Indian Ocean tsunami to the coast of Banda Aceh province in Indonesia. Few buildings remain standing and wreckage covers the streets.

The bike roared into life. George glanced at the shore and saw that the sea had drained away. He knew this was a sign that a tsunami was approaching. As they sped away from the beach, George glanced over his shoulder. He saw a line of towering waves approaching the shore, and behind them an even bigger wave. Seconds later the waves smashed onto the beach.

The second wave was taller than the palm trees on the shore. The trees splintered like matchsticks. As the bike raced for the hills, George saw cars and bodies swept along by the water. Most people had been fleeing when they were overtaken by the waves. As they reached the base of a hill, they were almost swept away by another wave approaching from the opposite direction. They scrambled to safety and watched terrified as water surged over the flat land below.

What caused the tsunamis?

The Indonesian earthquake struck at a deep trench on the ocean bed. The trench had formed where two plates pressed together and one was forced down below the other. The earthquake shifted and sloshed a huge mass of water. Tsunamis spread outward like giant ripples, racing across the ocean. Far out to sea the tsunamis formed relatively low waves, but they reared up to 78 feet high in the shallows as they struck the coast.

▲ An Indonesian woman covers her nose and mouth as she passes the bodies of tsunami victims laid out on a beach in the city of Banda Aceh. The bodies of the dead were laid out for identification before hasty burial, which was done to prevent the spread of disease. Relatives wept over loved ones while rescuers continued to scour the wreckage for victims.

▶ **Medical teams from many different nations flew into Banda Aceh following the tsunami disaster. They included doctors and medical students from South Korea, who set up two relief camps to treat the injured. Medical staff and rescuers reached remote villages by helicopter and, later, cars and trucks, when roads and bridges wrecked by the disaster had been repaired.**

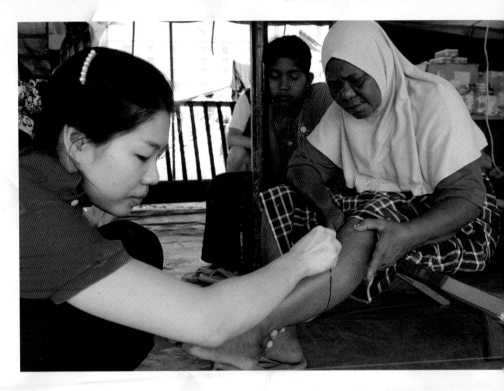

Tree trunks, cars, and boats acted like battering rams, smashing against houses. Then the waves sucked the debris with them as they swept back out to sea. When the water level dropped a little, George waded into the flood to rescue an old man, a woman, and two children. With his medical training he was able to revive three out of the four victims. But there were many bodies floating in the water.

When the water finally drained away, George left his friend and made his way home. Almost every building was flattened, and the streets were full of twisted wreckage. Very few trees were left standing. George's own house had been swept away. He managed to find a little food and returned to the hill to sleep. Small earthquakes were still shaking the ground and people screamed every time the earth shook.

The following day the first rescue helicopters arrived. George joined other survivors at an emergency camp where he helped to look after the injured. On hearing that he was a nurse, the rescuers asked George to join a medical team in a helicopter. The helicopter scoured the coast for survivors. From the helicopter George could see that the whole town had been flattened. Forests and fields had been swept away and even the shape of the coast had changed.

George continued with the rescue work for several weeks. He gave first aid, helped to clear the debris and bury the dead. He slept in a tent in the camp. After a few days aid packages began to arrive from abroad, containing food, clothing, tents, and medicine. These medical supplies were vital to George and other medical staff in their treatment of the tsunami victims.

Kusum's Story
Indian Ocean Tsunami, 2004

Tsunamis set off by the 2004 earthquake surged right across the Indian Ocean. They wrecked towns on the coasts of Thailand, India, and Sri Lanka. Around 800 people died when a train was swept off the tracks near the town of Galle in Sri Lanka. Kusum, a young teacher, was one of the survivors.

▲ Sri Lankan villagers look on at the wreckage of a train which was swept off its tracks by tsunamis in December 2004. The destructive waves were raised by the earthquake on the opposite side of the ocean. The train derailed near the town of Hikaduwa on Sri Lanka's southwest coast. The tsunamis killed at least 17,600 people in Sri Lanka alone.

The Indian Ocean disaster

The tsunamis traveled up to 2,983 miles across the ocean in the seven hours after the earthquake. They reached the distant coast of Somalia in East Africa where 300 people drowned. The earthquake and tsunamis killed a total of about 250,000 people—one of the worst disasters in living memory. No early warning system was in place to warn the countries around the ocean of the earthquake, so no alarm was given. Following the disaster sensors were set up to monitor undersea earthquakes that could trigger future tsunamis.

Kusum was a teacher in her early twenties who lived with her parents in the Sri Lankan capital, Colombo. On December 26 she took the early train from Colombo to Galle on the south coast. It was the start of a week's holiday, which she planned to spend with friends.

At around 10 a.m. the train stopped close to Galle. Kusum had taken a window seat to enjoy the view along the coastline. Now she heard screams outside and saw people running away from the shore. Through the trees she caught sight of huge waves racing up the beach. Moments later the waves swept the train off the tracks, separated the carriages, and tossed them inland.

Kusum's carriage was tilted but still upright. It started to fill with water. Through the window she could see another wave roaring towards them like a cliff of water. The wave pushed the carriage up against a house. People were panicking and trying to escape through the window. With water up to her neck, Kusum managed to scramble out and onto the roof of the house.

People still in the carriage were screaming. So many survivors had climbed onto the roof that it seemed likely to collapse. As the water level began to drop, Kusum left the roof and swam to dry land, using a wooden plank as a float.

Stumbling inland she met a woman who allowed her to shelter in her house. The phone lines were still working. Kusum telephoned her family to say she was safe. The next day she managed to get a bus back to Colombo using inland roads that had not been flooded. The capital was unharmed, but one of her friends in Galle had drowned. At home she watched news reports on television. Hundreds had died in the wrecked train, and Kusum felt very lucky to be alive.

Hua's Story
Chinese Earthquake, 2008

On May 12, 2008, a violent earthquake struck Sichuan province in the mountains of central China. The massive quake was felt in most parts of China. Over 50,000 people died. It was early afternoon, so most people were at work or school. Thousands of children died as schools collapsed. Hua, aged 11, survived and was helped by the Red Cross.

Hua lived with his grandmother in a town in Sichuan. His father had died when he was young. His mother could not find work locally, so she had moved to a city in the south to work in a factory. She visited Hua whenever she could. His grandmother worked in a factory part-time while Hua was at school.

Hua was in a math lesson when the earthquake struck. The children had been trained to hide under their desks in such a disaster, but everyone panicked and rushed outside. This was lucky as most of the school buildings collapsed. Many children and teachers were buried by the rubble. Hua escaped with a bad gash on his leg. Teachers and local people dug frantically in the ruins to try to free trapped children. After two hours rescue troops arrived. They shifted tons of rubble and brought out more children. But after the second day very few children were brought out alive.

▶ A mother weeps for her child among the ruins of Juyuan Middle School in Sichuan province in May 2008. The school collapsed when a severe earthquake struck the region, killing more than 900 students inside the flattened building. Over the whole of Sichuan province the earthquake claimed tens of thousands of lives, while many thousands more were injured.

▲ Victims of the Sichuan earthquake rest in an emergency camp in Mianyang in 2008. The camp held a total of 20,000 people. Disease can spread quickly in such overcrowded conditions. There was also a risk of mudslides and dam bursts throughout the quake struck region. Troops and medical teams responded promptly to the disaster, arriving on the scene within just a few hours.

The ground continued to shake as minor earthquakes struck. Everyone was nervous. Hua was taken to a rescue center set up by the Red Cross, where a doctor bandaged his leg. The staff was very kind. A woman arrived and told Hua that the factory where his grandmother worked had been badly damaged. She was among hundreds of people who were missing. That night Hua slept in a tent with blankets to keep him warm.

The following day the woman came back. She said Hua's grandmother had been found. She was in hospital with a head injury. Hua felt relieved. A few days later his mother arrived. She hugged Hua tightly. She said she would stay to look after them but they would have to remain in the camp because their house was in ruins. The school also had to be demolished and rebuilt. A European charity provided money to train more teachers, so the children could still have lessons even though there was no school.

Poor building standards

Hundreds of schools, factories, and offices collapsed during the Sichuan earthquake. In 1976 another severe earthquake had wrecked the Chinese city of Tangshan. Afterwards the government had introduced strict building standards so that new buildings would stand up better to earthquakes. However, in the 1990s China's economy grew very quickly and there was a building boom. Many new buildings did not meet the official standards. It was these new, cheaply built schools and offices that collapsed.

Peter's Story
North Sea Flood, 1953

On January 31, 1953, a severe storm hit northwest Europe at the same time as a very high tide. The two events produced widespread flooding in eastern Britain and the Netherlands. Canvey Island in the mouth of the Thames was one of the worst hit areas. Peter and his family lived on the island.

Canvey is a low-lying island in the Thames estuary. It was reclaimed from the sea in the 17th century. The island was at risk of flooding, but the sea defenses had been strengthened during World War II. Peter's family moved to the island after the war because the part of London where they lived had been badly bombed. At 15 Peter was the oldest of four brothers. His baby sister, Elsie, was just two.

The family's wooden bungalow stood in an exposed position just 328 feet from the sea wall. On January 31 a news report on the radio warned that a severe gale had raged across Scotland and was now heading south along Britain's east coast. A very high tide was also expected.

The storm and swollen seas hit Canvey at around 1 a.m. The high tide swept over the sea wall and through the streets. Peter woke up in the dead of night. He stepped out of bed and up to his knees in water. The house was in complete darkness. The storm was raging and he could hear the sound of roaring water.

The North Sea floods

The storm of 1953 produced the worst flooding for many years. In Britain 300 people drowned, including 58 people on Canvey. The low pressure storm sucked up water. As it swept south, gale force winds drove the mound of water down the narrow channel between Britain and Holland. The storm and high tide combined to produce sea levels 16 feet higher than normal. There were no weather satellites or computers in 1953, so experts could not predict the exact path of the storm. With telephone lines down and no radio broadcasts at night, there was no way of raising the alarm.

Peter woke the others. The floodwaters were rising quickly. Peter's father could not swim, but he used a chair to smash a hole in the ceiling so that the family could climb up into the rafters. Peter's mother stayed below, holding onto Elsie's baby carriage, which was in danger of floating away. After a while Peter lowered himself into the water to help his mother. The freezing water was now up to his chest.

The family sang hymns to keep their spirits up. The night seemed to last

▶ A row boat evacuates a family from their home on Canvey Island following the flood of January 31, 1953. This low-lying island in the Thames estuary was inundated after a severe storm and high tide breached local flood defenses. Flood waters covered the island for several days afterwards.

forever. Peter became numb. Everything was wet, and there was nothing to protect the baby from the cold. At some point Elsie stopped crying, but Peter and his mother still held onto the carriage.

Eventually dawn broke. Around 9 a.m. they heard a shout. Help had arrived in the form of a row boat. But the rower explained he could only take the dead. Elsie's small body was handed out of the window.

The floodwaters had gone down a little. The family was able to wade out of the house and clamber onto the sea wall. From here Peter could see that the whole island was flooded. Battling against a strong wind, they crossed the bridge to the mainland. They were then directed to a house on a small hill.

At the house they were given a hot drink and blankets. For two days they sheltered in a school. When the floods went down, they returned to Canvey to salvage their belongings. The whole island had been evacuated. Eventually the sea defenses were rebuilt, and people could move back if they chose. But Peter's family never got over the loss of Elsie. They left the island for good and started a new life in London.

Floods in Holland

The flooding was even worse in the Netherlands, much of which is actually below sea level. There the sea is kept back by high walls called dykes. In 1953 high seas broke through hundreds of dykes. Water surged as far as 37 miles inland and 1,800 people died. Following the disaster the Dutch built a major new flood defense system. It took 40 years to complete.

▲ Floodwaters cover a town and farmland in the Netherlands in January 1953. The effects of the North Sea flood were more severe here because much of the country is extremely low-lying. The floods breached 89 dykes in the Netherlands and covered 1,243 miles of land reclaimed from the sea. Some 46,000 homes were flooded, compared to 24,000 homes in Britain.

Jerry's Story
Mississippi Flood, 1993

In the summer of 1993 the Mississippi River in the southern United States burst its banks. Floodwater covered 75 towns and 30,888 square miles of land. Over 30,000 homes were swamped. Jerry, aged 18, and his family were among the flood victims.

Jerry's parents owned a pig farm by the Illinois River, which flows into the Mississippi. Jerry worked on the farm, which lay in a low-lying area called the Bottoms. A high bank called a levee had been built to contain the river. But in late June 1993, after months of heavy rain, water threatened to spill over the levee. Jerry and his family stripped the ground floor of their farmhouse and moved everything upstairs. They secured the pigs in a pen in the top field. They piled possessions into their truck and moved to a cousin's farm on a nearby hill.

By day, Jerry and his father returned to the Bottoms. They fed the pigs and helped neighbors stack sandbags to increase the height of the levee. But still the rain fell. On July 18 the river broke through the levee and surged across the fields. Jerry watched as the water crept towards the farm and then slowly rose to the height of the first floor window. The family returned by boat to rescue photo albums, Jerry's violin and other treasured possessions. Jerry and his dad herded the pigs to a neighbor's farm up the hill.

The rain continued. In mid-July the US president declared the Mississippi a disaster zone. The town across the river was flooded, along with many others. Jerry's father said that new houses that had been built right by the river should not have been allowed. The floodwaters even threatened the city of St Louis downstream, but the flood defenses held there. News reports said that the floods were the worst since the Great Flood of 1927, which had struck the Lower Mississippi.

The floodwater lingered for weeks. Finally, in early August, the rain stopped and the water level slowly started to drop. By late August

Causes of the Mississippi flood

The floods of 1993 followed a wet autumn and snowy winter the previous year. In spring melted snow swelled the river. Rain began to fall in March and continued for months. Following the Great Flood of 1927, levees had been built along the Mississippi and its tributaries to contain the water. However, some experts said the floods would have caused less damage had the levees been built to release water slowly, not hold it back. Some riverside towns had to be abandoned after the 1993 floods.

▲ In July 1993 residents of towns along the Mississippi River stacked sandbags to try to prevent their homes from flooding. Often their attempts were unsuccessful. Here the brown floodwaters have breached the temporary barrier to invade homes in a suburb of St Louis.

Jerry's family was able to return home. They worked hard to clear the black, stinking mud from their home, but decided eventually to abandon the old house. Using savings and flood insurance, they bought a new plot of land on the hill and rebuilt the farm there. Only the pigs still live down on the Bottoms.

Manuela's Story
Jarrell Tornado, 1997

Tornadoes are whirling funnels of air that sometimes form during thunderstorms. On May 27, 1997, an incredibly powerful tornado wrecked the small town of Jarrell, Texas. Eleven-year-old Manuela was among the survivors.

Manuela lived with her parents and younger brother in Jarrell. The morning of May 27 was very hot and humid. The forecast warned of thunderstorms. By mid-afternoon, towering black thunderclouds could be seen to the north. Manuela arrived home from school and was playing with her brother in the yard when their mother called them inside. A local news report warned that tornadoes had been sighted around Jarrell. A siren began to wail.

Manuela's parents had witnessed the destruction when a powerful tornado struck the area in 1989. When they built their home, they had dug a cellar below it and lined it with concrete. Now Manuela, her mother and brother rushed into the cellar and slammed the hatch. Their father was at work in the nearby city of Austin.

▶ A tornado snakes across farmland in the United States. Tornadoes are also called twisters. They contain the strongest winds in the world. The Jarrell tornado was one of a group of 11 that formed in the region that day. A group of tornadoes is called a swarm.

As they crouched in the darkness, they heard a roar like a jet engine getting louder and louder. Then came an incredible crashing and splintering and the sound of torrential rain. The noise continued for about 20 minutes. The family prayed as Manuela's mother clung to the hatch to keep it shut.

Finally the roaring died down. When all was quiet, they climbed out to find a scene of utter devastation. Their home was a heap of smashed wood, concrete blocks, and debris. They could see that other houses in the street had also been flattened. Just the concrete foundations remained.

What are tornadoes?

Tornadoes form below thunderclouds in hot, sticky weather. Warm, moist air begins to spiral upward. A spinning funnel reaches down from the cloud. When it touches the ground, it acts like a giant vacuum cleaner, sucking up debris. Tornadoes are just over half a mile across but can contain winds spinning at over 250 mph. Most last only a few minutes and weave across the landscape leaving a trail of debris. But the Jarrell tornado hovered over the town for about 20 minutes. The result was total destruction.

There was a screech of tires. Manuela's father drove up in his truck. He leapt out and hugged his family close. In the days after the disaster the family sheltered in a local school where they were given food, water, and clothing.

They had lost their house and all their possessions. However, they counted themselves lucky. Many people in the neighborhood had died, including some of Manuela's classmates. The family was safe, which was what mattered. For nine months they lived in a trailer while their home was rebuilt using a government grant. When it was finally ready, they moved back in.

◄ This aerial view shows the destruction caused by a tornado in the central United States. Experts believe that the Jarrell tornado contained incredibly powerful winds whirling at over 200 mph. It left a trail of destruction five miles long and almost half a mile wide.

Steve's Story
Rocky Mountains Avalanche, 1998

Avalanches occur in snowy mountains when a mass of snow breaks loose and hurtles down the steep slopes. The cascading snow can sweep away people, trees, and houses. In 1998 Steve was caught by an avalanche while on a hiking trip with his friend Joel.

▲ A massive avalanche roars down the slopes of Manaslu, one of the highest mountains in the Himalayas. Heavy snowfall and a steep gradient increase the risk of avalanche on slopes like these. If an avalanche occurs on the lower slopes of a mountain, it can wipe out forests and any settlements in its path.

What triggers avalanches?

Avalanches can be triggered by heavy rain or snowfall. A strong gust of wind or vibrations set up by a passing skier or hiker can set a mass of snow in motion. So can a thaw. When meltwater seeps through the snow, it forms a slippery layer that makes the snow unstable. These so-called wet-snow avalanches are common in spring.

Steve and Joel were university students and keen climbers. They had just finished their end-of-year exams and decided to celebrate by going hiking. Their goal was a snow-covered peak high in the Rocky Mountains in the western United States. They drove into the mountains in the evening and spent a cold night in the car. They began their climb before dawn.

The weather was fine but windy. It was spring and thick snow covered the upper slopes. As the Sun rose, the snow partly melted. Slushy snow slowed them down and it was five hours before they reached the summit ridge. Joel and Steve had planned to make a quick descent by sliding down the upper snowfields—a technique they had used before. Now Joel expressed his worry that the slushy conditions could trigger an avalanche.

Steve felt confident that an avalanche was unlikely. He leapt off the ridge onto the snowfield, only to sink up to his waist in wet snow. As he struggled to free himself, he heard a loud ripping sound. A large crack spread right across the snowfield and the whole slope avalanched.

Steve was catapulted down the slope into a narrow gully and onto jagged rocks below. One of his feet caught among the rocks and he heard something snap.

Luckily the avalanche now slowed and stopped. Steve lay at the surface 1,312 feet below the ridge. He tried to stand but his ankle was broken. From the ridge high above, Joel spotted his friend's blue jacket. He saw him wave and realized that he was conscious, but injured. Joel knew that if he tried to climb down to Steve he could trigger another avalanche. He waved back and then ran down back the mountain the way they had come.

Tripping and stumbling, Joel reached the car in less than an hour. He raced downhill to a police station in the valley where he raised the alarm. However, the windy conditions made it unsafe to launch a helicopter rescue until late afternoon. It was almost dark before the rescuers managed to winch Steve to safety. After weeks in plaster and months of painful exercises, Steve was able to walk again. Eventually he returned to hiking, but he now takes great care on snowy slopes.

Joe's Story
Hurricane Katrina, 2005

In August 2005 a violent hurricane struck the coast of the southern United States. Hurricane Katrina whipped up high seas that breached flood defenses and swamped the city of New Orleans. Eighty percent of the city flooded and 1,000 people died. Joe, aged 16, was among thousands who were evacuated from the stricken city.

Joe lived with his parents and sister in a single-story house in New Orleans. His grandmother lived in a two-story house nearby. On August 25, 2005, Joe heard on the news that a powerful hurricane named Katrina had struck Florida and was heading west across the Gulf of Mexico.

▼ A United States Air Force sergeant looks down from an Air Force helicopter, scanning the flooded streets of New Orleans for survivors. United States Air Force teams were credited with rescuing more than a thousand people from the city in the wake of Hurricane Katrina.

New Orleans, located on the Mississippi near the Gulf Coast, was at risk of flooding. Experts warned that the city's flood defenses might not hold if the storm passed directly overhead. On August 28 the authorities ordered the evacuation of New Orleans. Thousands of people left by car, but Joe's family did not own a car. Bus and train services were swamped by the huge numbers of people trying to leave the city. Joe's parents decided to stay and try to ride out the storm.

On August 29 Katrina struck the coast near New Orleans. The hurricane caused an extra-high tide that broke through the levees guarding the city. Floodwater surged through the streets, and buses and trains stopped running. Everyone who had not already left was trapped.

When Joe's home was flooded, the family took refuge in his grandmother's house. The first day the water was clear. Joe and his sister even went swimming. But the water soon became murky and polluted with oil and sewage. Water supplies were cut off so toilets stopped working. There was no power. On the third day the family's food and water ran out. Joe and his father waded as far as the local store, whose windows had been smashed. They took water and canned food to keep the family going.

By the fifth day black, stinking water surrounded the house. Joe's parents realized they had to leave. Clutching a few possessions, they waded through thigh-deep water to a local bridge where a boat took them to an emergency shelter. From there a bus took them to the airport. After a day at the airport, Joe and his dad were flown to Washington, DC, where they were sent to a sports stadium called the Armory. Joe's mother, grandmother, and sister were sent to a stadium in Houston, Texas.

At the Armory Joe was given food, water, and fresh clothes. He slept in a dormitory. It was noisy, but conditions were better than in Houston. His sister phoned to report that the stadium there was overcrowded, with not enough water and poor sanitation. In mid-September Joe was told he could attend a high school in Washington. He stayed to complete a year of school there. Meanwhile, back in New Orleans, troops and rescue services pumped stinking water out of the city and began repairing the levees. Water and electricity supplies were restored, and cleaning and repair work began.

In Washington the teachers and students were kind and understanding. But their questions made Joe feel he was on show in a museum. The television continued to show reports of New Orleans, but Joe could not bear to watch them. They reminded him of dreadful things he had seen, such as a body floating in the water. At the end of the school year, Joe went home, and the family was reunited. But Joe's grandmother remained in Houston. She refused to return to the city that held such bad memories.

What are hurricanes?

Hurricanes are vast spinning storms. They have a similar structure to tornadoes but are many times larger, measuring up to 500 miles across. Katrina contained winds of over 175 mph. Hurricanes form over warm oceans when clashing winds start to spiral upwards. An area of low pressure in the center of the storm sucks up a mound of water called a storm surge. When Hurricane Katrina hit the Gulf Coast, the storm surge caused enormous damage. Emergency services failed to cope with the disaster in New Orleans. The US government was later criticized for its poor handling of the crisis.

▼ Evacuees from New Orleans were housed in the Astrodome, a stadium in Houston, Texas, before being sent to other emergency accommodation. With 16,000 people sheltering here, conditions were severely overcrowded. Many people felt that the authorities did not handle the crisis well.

Hasana's Story
Cyclone Sidr, 2007

In the Indian Ocean, hurricanes are called cyclones. Low-lying Bangladesh, on the shores of the Indian Ocean, has often been badly damaged by floods caused by these tropical storms. On November 15, 2007, Bangladesh was hit by Cyclone Sidr, the worst storm for a decade. Hasana was among tens of thousands of people made homeless by the storm.

Hasana, 13, lived with her parents, elder brother and aunt in a small village by the coast. Her father was a fisherman who kept his boat on the local lagoon. On November 14 the radio warned that a powerful cyclone had formed out at sea and was sweeping toward Bangladesh.

▲ These Bangladeshi women came from a village that was destroyed by Cyclone Sidr in November 2007. They have managed to salvage a few possessions. Their homes were wrecked when the cyclone roared through the village with winds of up to 150 mph. The severe storm caused sea levels to rise to around ten feet.

At risk of flooding

Bangladesh is one of the world's poorest countries. It is very densely populated. Three quarters of the country is less than ten feet above sea level. Most of Bangladesh consists of either low-lying land watered by two mighty rivers, the Ganges and Brahmaputra, or the vast, swampy deltas that have formed at the river mouths. This whole area is at risk of river floods as well as storm surges. In 1991 a storm surge washed over coasts and islands causing 140,000 deaths.

The family decided to take refuge in a storm shelter, which had been built on slightly higher ground away from the lagoon. The concrete shelter stood on stilts. Each family member could take only a few possessions. Hasana's father took his best net. Her mother took her cooking pots. Hasana took her school textbook. She was about to take her exams.

The storm hit the following night and raged for hours. High winds rocked the shelter. Torrential rainfall swelled local rivers, causing flooding. A storm surge from the cyclone washed right over the lagoon and village. When the storm passed, the family returned home to find the village destroyed. Their home had been washed away and their chickens and goat had drowned. Hasana helped her father and brother sift through the wreckage for materials to build a makeshift shelter. They stayed at a neighbor's house for several days.

Local water supplies were contaminated and power lines were down. Salt water had ruined the crops, so there was little food. The family was forced to go to an emergency center run by a European aid agency. There they were given food and water as well as blankets, matches, and plastic sheeting. The family's boat had been wrecked by the storm, so her father had no way of earning money. They had to survive on aid until her father could build a new boat.

Hasana's school had also been badly damaged. The aid organization established a temporary school for Hasana and the other pupils until the building was repaired. Three months later the school reopened. Hasana took her exams and passed with good marks.

Omar's Story
Drought in Ethiopia, 2008

A drought is a long period without rain. Many parts of Africa are regularly gripped by drought, but Ethiopia is one of the worst-affected areas. In 2008 drought struck here when the summer rains failed. Crops withered and animals died of thirst. Omar, 14, was one of many thousands of young people who were affected by the disaster.

Omar lived with his parents, younger brother, and sister in a village in southern Ethiopia. His father was a farmer and, as the eldest son, Omar worked alongside him. In spring 2008 Omar's father planted corn, but the crop died when the rains failed in June. Omar and his father worked on other local farms that still had water for crops. They spent their meager wages on cornmeal, which Omar's mother boiled with salted water to make porridge once a day. On some days there was no money to buy cornmeal. His mother just gave them hot, salted water.

In July Omar's father carried his little sister Marisa to a health center run by an aid organization. The center was more than 12 miles away. Marisa was six years old but so small and undernourished she looked about three. At the center Marisa was given high-energy food and medicine. When the aid workers brought her home a week later, her mother cried. She said she had not expected to see Marisa alive.

◀ A farmer and his children plant bean seeds in a field in southern Ethiopia. This part of Africa is often hit by drought. Most natural disasters are sudden and relatively short-lived, but droughts can last for months or even years. Sometimes when the rains do finally come, they cause destructive floods. This was the case in 2007.

▲ A grandmother mourns the death of her granddaughter in the intensive care unit of a medical center in Ethiopia. She is comforted by mothers holding their babies. The grandmother had cared for her grandchild for two years following the death of the girl's mother. The women are being looked after by an international medical and aid organization.

But life was still a great struggle. There was now very little work in the area, and almost everyone was suffering. Omar and his family had to rely on help from charities as drought conditions continued for months.

The organization that helped Omar's family had worked in the region since 1974. It provided food, water, and medical supplies to families like Omar's that were in danger of starvation. It also provided farm equipment and dug wells. It gave advice on new farming methods and offered training so local people could help themselves. In summer 2008 the charity estimated that 750,000 local children were, like Marisa, at risk of malnutrition. Omar's father was among tens of thousands of poor farmers badly affected by drought.

History of drought in Ethiopia

Ethiopia is a mainly mountainous country in East Africa. For much of the year the climate is very dry, but a short rainy season, which begins in June, allows crops to grow. In a good year the rains last until September, but in a bad year, they don't come at all. In 1981–5 four years of drought coincided with a civil war that also disrupted farming. Tens of thousands of people abandoned their homes and fled to refugee centers. Many died on the way. When international reporters spread news of the disaster, people around the world gave money to ease the suffering.

Hannah's Story
Australian Bushfires, 2009

Drought and heatwaves can spark wildfires in hot, dry countries such as Australia. In high winds fire can spread quickly. In February 2009 the worst bushfires in Australian history swept the southern state of Victoria. The town of Kinglake near Melbourne was destroyed. Hannah was one of the survivors.

Hannah, 16, lived in Kinglake with her parents and dog Jimmy. In February 2009, the height of summer in Australia, a long drought had made streams and reservoirs low. Now a heatwave and strong winds produced a high risk of bushfire. On February 7 a power line snapped by the wind sparked a fire in a plantation near Kinglake.

Northwesterly winds spread the flames, creating a long, narrow band of fire running east through the suburbs. Hannah and her parents watched firefighters tackle the blaze on television. At around 6 p.m. the wind veered southwest and grew even stronger. The long ribbon of fire became a firefront that swept north through town.

No one realized how close the fire had crept until they heard a roar. They rushed outside and saw houses down the street blazing. Hannah's father turned on the sprinkler system on the roof. Their car stood outside but with fires now burning all around them they did not know which way to go.

▶ A wildfire races up a deep gully near the town of Kinglake, about 60 miles northeast of Melbourne. The bushfires, which started on February 7, 2009, were the deadliest in Australian history. A total of 1,740 square miles of land were burned. The fires were sparked following a record dry spell.

▶ A couple stand in the ruins of their house in Kinglake. Their home was utterly destroyed when fire swept the town in February 2009. The Kinglake fire was the most destructive of all the bushfires in the region. A total of 120 people died.

Strong winds scattered sparks through the air. The house next door caught fire. Hannah and her parents took refuge in their swimming pool. Hannah held tight to Jimmy's collar. Then they heard a helicopter. A policeman appeared out of the smoke, swinging on a line from the helicopter. He jumped down and shouted at them to get into their car. The helicopter would show them which way to go.

Hannah and her dad bundled into the car with the policeman. Hannah still had Jimmy. Her mother got into the car behind with their elderly neighbors. Using his shortwave radio to talk to the helicopter, the policeman directed them onto a back road. When they stopped a short distance away, Hannah saw that her whole street was burning.

They spent the night in a hotel in a nearby town. In the morning they returned to find the sprinkler system had saved their house. But most houses in the street had burned down and some neighbors had died. Hannah's family invited their elderly neighbors to stay while their home was rebuilt using insurance money.

Bushfires in Australia

The Kinglake fire was just one of 400 separate fires that burned in Victoria in February 2009. Some were sparked by fallen power lines, other by lightning strikes. Some were started deliberately—this is called arson. A total of 173 people died and 78 towns were damaged. Despite the efforts of 60,000 firefighters, the last of the fires were not extinguished until March 14.

Glossary

aftermath The period following an event such as a natural disaster.

arson When someone starts a fire deliberately.

bushfire The word for a forest fire or wildfire in Australia.

crater lake A lake that forms in the hollow crater of a volcano.

crust Earth's outer layer.

cyclone A tropical storm, also called a hurricane.

dam A structure built to hold back water.

decade A period of ten years.

delta An area of low, swampy land at a river's mouth, built up from sediment dropped by the river as it reaches the sea.

demolish Tear down a building.

disrupt Disturb.

donation A gift, usually of money.

drought A long period without rain.

estuary The lower part of a river, near the mouth.

evacuation When everyone is ordered to leave an area because of danger.

extinguish Put out a fire.

famine When many people go hungry because food is scarce. Many famines are caused by drought.

fault A deep crack in the rocks at Earth's surface. Faults often occur along the borders between two tectonic plates.

focus The point at which an earthquake strikes deep underground.

gale A very strong wind.

humid Moist.

lagoon A lake by the sea.

lahar A volcanic flow.

levee A high bank built along a river to contain the water, so that it does not flood the surrounding land.

malnutrition A condition caused by a shortage of healthy food.

mantle The thick, red-hot layer below Earth's outer crust.

meager Small.

molten Describes a solid that is so hot that it has become a liquid.

refugee A person who has been forced to leave his or her home because of danger, such as a natural disaster or war.

reservoir An artificial lake built to store water.

salvage Save something from wreckage.

sensor An instrument for measuring or recording. Some sensors are used to record earthquakes.

tectonic plate One of the enormous slabs of rock that make up Earth's outer layer or crust.

tremor A minor earthquake.

tsunami A towering wave set off when an earthquake, volcanic eruption, or landslide disturbs the ocean bed.

Further Information

Books

The DK Atlas of the World's Worst Natural Disasters by Lesley Newson (Dorling Kindersley, 1998)

DK Eyewitness: Natural Disasters by Claire Watts (Dorling Kindersley, 2006)

Natural Disasters: Floods by Chris Oxlade (Wayland, 2007)

Nature's Fury: Hurricane! by Anne Rooney (Franklin Watts, 2006)

Savage Planet by Liz McLeod (Granada Media, 2000)

Websites

earthquake.usgs.gov
United States Geological Survey site on earthquakes.

environment.nationalgeographic.com/environment/natural-disasters
National Geographic website on natural disasters.

www.savethechildren.org
The website of Save the Children, a charity helping children in need around the world.

serc.carleton.edu/NAGTWorkshops/ocean/visualizations/tsunami.html
Tsunami visualizations.

www.unicef.org.uk
The website of the United Nations Children's Fund—UNICEF.

volcano.oregonstate.edu
Information on volcanoes.

Index